FORGOTTEN FACTS ABOUT

PIONEER LIFE

BY KATHLEEN CONNORS

HISTORY'S FORGOTTEN FACTS

Enslow PUBLISHING

Please visit our website, www.enslow.com. For a free color catalog of all our high-quality books, call toll free 1-800-398-2504 or fax 1-877-980-4454.

Library of Congress Cataloging-in-Publication Data
Names: Connors, Kathleen, author.
Title: Forgotten facts about pioneer life / Kathleen Connors.
Description: Buffalo, New York : Enslow Publishing, [2024] | Series: History's forgotten facts | Includes bibliographical references and index.
Identifiers: LCCN 2023031738 | ISBN 9781978537828 (library binding) | ISBN 9781978537811 (paperback) | ISBN 9781978537835 (ebook)
Subjects: LCSH: Frontier and pioneer life–West (U.S.)–Juvenile literature. | West (U.S.)–Social life and customs–19th century–Juvenile literature. | West (U.S.)–Social life and customs–18th century–Juvenile literature.
Classification: LCC F596 .C7364 2024 | DDC 978/.02–dc23/eng/20230707
LC record available at https://lccn.loc.gov/2023031738

Published in 2024 by
Enslow Publishing
2544 Clinton Street
Buffalo, NY 14224

Portions of this work were originally authored by Kristen Rajczak and published as *Life as a Pioneer.* All new material in this edition authored by Kathleen Connors.

Designer: Tanya Dellaccio Keeney
Editor: Kristen Nelson

Photo credits: Cover, series background (banners) Ledelena/Shutterstock.com; cover, series background (paper) Vitaly Korovin/Shutterstock.com; cover, series background (wood) Pataradon Luangtongkum/Shutterstock.com; cover (main image) Grafissimo/iStock.com; pp. 5, 6, 13, 17 Everett Collection/Shutterstock.com; p. 7 Tony Baggett/Shutterstock.com; p. 9 (top) JNix/Shutterstock.com; p. 9 (bottom) Andy Sutherland/Shutterstock.com; p. 11 whitemay/iStock.com; p. 15 Courtesy of Library of Congress; p. 19 Deborah C/Shutterstock.com.

Printed in the United States of America

CPSIA compliance information: Batch #CWENS24: For further information contact Enslow Publishing at 1-800-398-2504.

CONTENTS

Words in the glossary appear in **bold** type the first time they are used in the text.

SETTLING THE FRONTIER

A pioneer is anyone who makes a discovery or finds a new way of doing something. During the 1700s and 1800s, groups of people we now call pioneers headed to the American **frontier**. They were drawn there by the promise of land or a new start.

The pioneers journeyed west. Some headed across the Appalachian Mountains to places including present-day Kentucky. Others traveled even farther and made the hard trip across the Great Plains.

ONCE PIONEERS FOUND A PLACE TO SETTLE, THEY HAD A LOT TO OVERCOME. SOME PEOPLE DIDN'T STAY LONG OUT THERE BECAUSE LIFE WAS SO HARD!

DON'T FORGET!

In 1862, the U.S. government passed the **Homestead Act**. This act granted land to those willing to farm it for five years. They only had to pay a small fee.

GOING IN A GROUP

Around 1750, big groups began to travel west together on horseback or by wagon. These pioneers were often members of the same family and people from the same area.

DON'T FORGET!

Some of the earliest pioneers were men **exploring** the land or fur trappers.

Journeying with a big group had many advantages. They could carry more supplies and help each other if a wagon wheel broke or a river was hard to cross. Pioneers also thought about safety. A big group meant more people to guard against Native American attacks.

ONE OF THE MAIN **ROUTES** PIONEERS TRAVELED WAS THE OREGON TRAIL. IT STARTED IN MISSOURI AND ENDED IN OREGON TERRITORY.

CHALLENGES AT THE START

To the pioneers, the frontier seemed to be a wild, unsettled place. However, Native Americans had been living in many areas for thousands of years. In fact, the pioneers often settled on Native American land! That's why pioneers faced attacks from local Native groups.

Problems with Native Americans was just one challenge pioneers faced. After their long journey, pioneers had to find food and water. They began the hard work of clearing their new land for farming.

DURING THE 1830S, THE U.S. GOVERNMENT FORCED THE CREEK, CHOCTAW, CHICKASAW, AND CHEROKEE TO MOVE FROM THEIR LAND TO INDIAN TERRITORY IN PRESENT-DAY OKLAHOMA. THE CHEROKEE REMOVAL IS CALLED THE TRAIL OF TEARS.

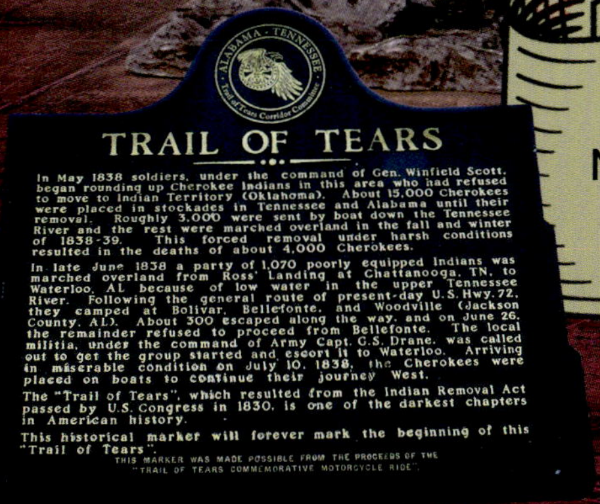

DON'T FORGET!

Native American groups gave up some land through **treaties**. But, as more pioneers went west, Native Americans were forced off even more of their land.

A HOUSE MAKES A HOME?

Sometimes, pioneers lived out of their wagons or tents for weeks after they arrived! Then, the first homes pioneers built were little more than **shacks** that didn't keep out cold, wind, or rain.

Pioneers on the Great Plains used sod, or mud and grass, to build "soddies." These weren't much more than covered holes in the ground. The **temporary** homes pioneers built led to living conditions that were hard for many to bear.

MANY PIONEER FAMILIES DIDN'T SPEND THE TIME TO BUILD **PERMANENT** HOMES, SUCH AS A LOG CABIN, UNTIL THEY KNEW THEY WERE GOING TO STAY.

DON'T FORGET!

Pioneers used newspapers as wallpaper and toilet paper!

GROWING SEASON

The first few years on the frontier were trying. Pioneers cleared land, prepared soil for planting, and tended crops. Farmers hoped for a good **harvest**, but that didn't always happen.

In addition to the crops grown to sell, pioneers planted kitchen gardens in the spring and fall. These fruits and vegetables were an important part of the pioneer **diet**. The garden harvest was often dried or jarred for use during winter when fresh foods were hard to find.

DON'T FORGET!

Some farmers used a team of oxen, or a kind of male cow, to clear their land.

PIONEERS—AND THEIR CROPS—FACED HEAT, ICY WINTERS, AND DUST STORMS, DEPENDING ON WHERE THEY SETTLED.

HUNTING

Many pioneer men hunted the meat their families ate. They may have hunted duck, turkey, and rabbit, and caught fish, depending on where they lived. The meat had to be prepared right away. In the summer, fresh meat could begin to rot in a few hours! Often, pioneers roasted, or cooked, the meat. They used salt to **preserve** meat too.

Most people lived too far from a general store to buy supplies regularly. Pioneer families often had to make do with what was on hand.

DON'T FORGET!

Pioneers might only travel "to town" once or twice a year to gather what they needed and to send or receive mail.

PIONEER MEALS MIGHT HAVE INCLUDED WILD TURKEY, SHOWN HERE.

PIONEER CLOTHES

On the frontier, pioneers didn't have much clothing. A pioneer woman might have only two or three dresses in all! In some areas, there wasn't cloth around to make more clothing. Then, pioneer women had to make their own cloth.

DON'T FORGET!

Pioneers did **laundry** by hand. They had to gather water, heat it, and make laundry soap in order to get their few clothes clean. The chore could take all day!

MANY PIONEERS COULDN'T AFFORD BRIGHTLY COLORED DYES OR CLOTH OTHER THAN WOOL.

While most men wore breeches—a kind of short pant—during the 18th century, pioneer men wore long pants to keep themselves covered in the fields. Before this, only shepherds and sailors wore long pants!

CHILDHOOD ON THE FRONTIER

Children on the frontier worked hard to help their families. They brought water in from the well or milked cows and collected eggs if their family owned livestock.

Both girls and boys started working on the family farm at about 10 years old. Girls in other parts of the country didn't work outside the house much during the 1700s and 1800s. However, since pioneer women needed to rope cattle as well as keep house, girls learned to do both.

IF A PIONEER COMMUNITY HAD A SCHOOLHOUSE, IT COMMONLY HAD ONE ROOM FOR STUDENTS OF ALL AGES. SOME CHILDREN HAD NO BOOKS TO LEARN FROM. OTHERS HAD ONLY THE FAMILY BIBLE.

DON'T FORGET!

Until they were old enough to work in the fields, young pioneer children helped around the house by sewing, cooking, and doing laundry.

WORRIES AND FUN

For pioneers, illness was a common worry. There were few doctors, and they had to ride many miles between small frontier homesteads to help those who were sick or hurt.

Still, there was time for fun on the frontier! Neighbors made cheese together. Groups held spelling bees at the schoolhouse. Pioneer communities hosted picnics and dances in the summer. Songs such as "Home on the Range" and "Skip to My Lou" were popular for the pioneers to sing and dance to!

DON'T FORGET!

Medicine wasn't always available or affordable. Frontier doctors had to learn how to use plants to treat illnesses, aches, and pains.

FAMOUS PIONEERS

LAURA INGALLS WILDER
WRITER WHO GREW UP ON THE FRONTIER AND WROTE ABOUT HER LIFE IN THE *LITTLE HOUSE ON THE PRAIRIE* SERIES

MERIWETHER LEWIS AND WILLIAM CLARK
LED A GROUP TO EXPLORE THE FRONTIER ALL THE WAY TO THE PACIFIC NORTHWEST

BRIGHAM YOUNG
BROUGHT MEMBERS OF THE CHURCH OF JESUS CHRIST OF LATTER-DAY SAINTS TO THE SITE OF SALT LAKE CITY, IN TODAY'S UTAH

JULIETTE AUGUSTA MAGILL KINZIE
WRITER WHO TOLD ABOUT THE GROWTH OF THE MIDWEST AND TREATMENT OF NATIVE AMERICANS DURING THE MID-1800S

DANIEL BOONE
HELPED FIND A WAY THROUGH THE CUMBERLAND GAP, AIDING FUTURE PIONEERS ACROSS THE APPALACHIAN MOUNTAINS

GLOSSARY

diet: The food and drink a person eats.

explore: To search in order to find out new things.

frontier: The edge of a settled part of a country.

harvest: The crop grown in a field or garden.

homestead: The home and land received from the U.S. government.

laundry: Clothes to be washed.

medicine: A drug taken to make a sick person well.

permanent: Meant to last a long time.

preserve: To keep from rotting.

route: A course that people travel.

shack: A small, roughly built shelter.

temporary: Meant to be used for a short amount of time.

treaty: An agreement between groups.

FOR MORE INFORMATION

Books

Goss, Elizabeth Ames. *My Way West: Real Kids Traveling the Oregon and California Trails*. Berkeley, CA: West Margin Press, 2021.

Quick, Megan. *How Did Pioneer Kids Live?* Buffalo, NY: Enslow Publishing, 2024.

Websites

A Day in the Life of a Pioneer Child
https://www.jobcarrmuseum.org/blog/a-day-in-the-life-of-a-pioneer-child-morning-routines-tacoma-in-the-1870s
Find out about the daily life of pioneer kids during the 1800s, as well as other information.

History at Home
https://www.thehistorycenter.org/wp-content/uploads/2020/04/March2020-History-at-Home-Pioneer2.pdf
Read more about being a pioneer and find a fun activity to do at home.

Publisher's note to educators and parents: Our editors have carefully reviewed these websites to ensure that they are suitable for students. Many websites change frequently, however, and we cannot guarantee that a site's future contents will continue to meet our high standards of quality and educational value. Be advised that students should be closely supervised whenever they access the internet.

INDEX